Inside The Bubble

Lessons Learned from a Life in Business and Protective Services

Mark "Six" James

Inside The Bubble
Lessons Learned from a Life in Business and Protective Services
Mark "Six" James

Published by Samurai Publishing, Atlanta, Georgia

Editor: Carla Dupont-Huger - Write with Carla

Cover Photo: Afrika Pratt-Ansa

Ordering Information
For additional copies contact your favorite bookstore or email info@pantherprotectionservices.com. Quantity discounts available.

ISBN
13 digit: 978–0–9976795-0-2   10 digit: 0-9976795-0-6

What the readers are saying

"I highly recommend Inside the Bubble as a must read. What I like about the book, is its refreshing approach to the total leader. The value driven approach is timely and greatly needed."

Leslie Smith, IBM, North America Software Marketing Manager

"What I really like about Inside the Bubble is that it provides insights into the inner workings of the business environment but challenges individuals to think OUTSIDE the bubble, to truly garner a real VISION!"

Gentry Humphrey, Nike Vice President Footwear (Retired)

"Mark James has done an excellent job of capturing the secret sauce of living a full and successful life. The tenet of simplicity is true in business leadership as well as in our life's journey."

Darryl Thomas, President/Franchise Owner b's Mongolian Grill

"Inside the Bubble, is a breath of fresh air, it provides rock solid business and leadership practices in a straight forward easy to read format that you can incorporate in action immediately."

Trevor Harvey, Student Development Advisor, State College of Florida

"It is clear that Mark James has had the benefit of having a front row seat and first hand business experience of the keys to success in high powered positions. Through this book I am able to learn from what has clearly been proven to work and adapt my own approach to achieve success both personally and professionally."

Elizabeth Thompson, Diabetes Care Specialist, Novo Nordisk

"Mark is one of the thought leaders in our space who always lets his actions precede his voice. When you lead from the front you not only garner respect, you inspire confidence in others. Inside the bubble is a synthesis of lessons he has learned in the world as a business executive and the protection world safeguarding high net-worth individuals and how those life lessons can translate to make an individual more successful in achieving their personal and professional goals."

Elijah Shaw, CEO, ICON Services

"I had the pleasure of working alongside Mark during his days as a General Manager at Nike. He brought a contagious passion for success and a professional account management strategy that successfully leveraged the Nike brand, product, and marketing support. He took the Sales Team from managing relationships to real brand management and healthy revenue/brand growth. Mark shares many of his keys to success in Inside the Bubble."

Rogers James, Managing Director, 3E Business Consulting

TABLE OF CONTENTS

What the Readers Are Saying   IV

Dedication   VII

About the Author   VIII

Introduction   XI

Six on Business   1

Six on Leadership   57

Six on Life   81

Six on the Things That Really Matter   100

Index   120

Appendix   125

My Personal Action Plan   126

DEDICATION

To Grandma Mary Emma, Daddy Jack,
Grandma McElroy, Mom, Dad, Renee, Carla
and Jasmyne thank you for your leadership, wisdom and
demonstrated acts of compassion and humanity, that you
have shown through the years. Because of each of you, I
stand on strong shoulders, and it continues to inspire me to
try to make a difference in the lives of others.

About the Author

As a former corporate executive and performance consultant to Fortune 500 companies and now executive director of a full service protection agency, Mark has had the pleasure of sitting in the rear seat of the VIP vehicle, as well as the front right seat as a protection specialist securing the safety of dignitaries and high net-worth individuals. During that time he has had the opportunity to see first-hand the common threads shared by highly successful leaders and high performing organizations. Through "Inside the Bubble," Mark shares his insights on business, leadership, life and the things that really matter to help the readers achieve growth through focus and balance. Most long term successful careers are built on personal strengths used by people who enjoy what they do. That philosophy was the catalyst that fueled his transition from the traditional business world of corporate America into entrepreneurship and protective services. He is an internationally published author and keynote speaker.

Prior to starting Panther Protection Services, Mark was president and CEO of The Renmark Group a sales consultancy, which focused on helping organizations build their organizational competencies around revenue generation, through enhancing customer relationships, selling skill development, strategic recruiting and benchmarking of their customer management teams.

Prior to the Renmark Group he spent the previous 23 years specializing in building top performing customer management organizations. With a distinguished reputation in sales and marketing leadership, Mark has worked with such industry giants as Miller Heiman, Nike, Coca-Cola and Sea-Land Services. Mark has held such positions as Executive Vice President/Chief Sales Officer, General Manager, Regional Director, Market Development Manager and numerous other leadership positions.

Having managed annual revenues in excess of a quarter of a billion dollars, he has built successful client engagement strategies, created joint client marketing initiatives, overseen global, national and regional sales organizations, as well as developed enterprise wide training initiatives.

Through The Renmark Group, Mark leveraged his expertise by helping his clients accelerate revenue growth, build and grow client relationships, in addition to coaching and developing their people.

Throughout his career, Mark expanded the market, increased market share, penetration, increased revenues, while improving customer satisfaction.

INTRODUCTION

In protective services the term *inside the bubble* refers to the inner workings of the President of the United States inner circle. It is the operations hub of the activity. Through my book "Inside the Bubble," I go back to my roots of business and leadership to provide you a peak under the tent of the common threads shared by highly successful leaders and high performing organizations. While the industries may change, the fundamental factors of success remain constant.

When you peel back the onion and take away style, bravado and illusion, great leaders all share a common foundation. That foundation is built on vision, inspiration, and execution. The common mortar that holds that platform together is "simplicity as a standard." However, one fundamental trait that I found absent from many was rejuvenation.

Through the years, I have witnessed many executives who were great at running organizations, but horrible adding value at home. Others delivered phenomenal business results but left a series of body bags along the way. Without some level of balance in their lives, many become victims of their own success and it manifests itself in ulcers, high blood pressure, strokes, heart attacks and other stress related illnesses coupled with estranged family relationships and divorces. Value-driven leadership doesn't mean you tolerate underperformance, it just means excellence can be achieved with balance and inspiration and doesn't require intimidation to garner results. I don't believe success and performance have to be punishing for either the leader, their employees or their families. This is my humble attempt at helping existing and inspiring leaders bridge that gap.

This book is part inspiration, part motivation, part perspiration and a hell of a lot confession. Unless you have clarity in vision, you can never inspire others to follow. People don't mind being led, as long as they know you understand where you are going. Vision always precedes inspiration. Thus vision is the only real superpower.

To quote John F. Kennedy, *"Efforts and courage are not enough without purpose and direction."*

Purpose and direction are magnified by inspiration. As a leader, your job is to make your actions scale. You are no longer a doer parse, you are an enabler of doers that is your force multiplier. From my days in corporate America, as an executive vice president, I used to sit down with my leadership team and ask, "If I told you, you now have unlimited resources and I will fund anything you request as long as you would either maximize our ability to grow our revenues double digit or significantly enhance client satisfaction, what would you ask for?" As a business leader, you should be prepared to entertain those offers, if you can get the appropriate return on your investment. If you want exponential growth you have to start by doing exponential things. It starts by first removing the obstacles to success which are impeding exponential growth. That starts with first inspiring your team to think big.

When it comes to execution, the simpler you can make things the easier it is to execute them. I remember one day, I was teaching defensive tactics at a bodyguard training academy. I always start by informing the students that engagement is not our objective; courtesy and diplomacy are our greatest assets and an escape beats an encounter every time. I inform them if we cannot evacuate and we are forced to engage, things must be efficient because if you are engaging – your client is unprotected. Then a student approached me saying, "I wrestled in college and I can hold my own."

"Protective services is not about wrestling," I responded.

"But you don't understand, I wrestled for three years in college and lettered all three years."

I smiled and said, "I understand."

He continued, "What would you do if someone grabbed you like this?" He then grabbed me by the arm and shoulders and proceeded to attempt to wrestle me. I immediately put my thumb in his eye.

He turned me a loose immediately and yelled, "Ouch that hurt! What did you do that for?"

"I told you protective services is not about wrestling. My objective was for you to break contact and turn me a loose immediately, you did. Putting my thumb in your eye was the simplest must effective action that would bring about immediate results. It is also size and strength neutral. No matter how big the attacker or how small the person being attacked, it works," I answered. Simplicity is always the goal, how do you standardize the process so it works across the enterprise?

I recently received a call from one of my clients, who owns multiple casual theme restaurants, about helping them enhance their food and beverage strategies. Despite changes in consumer taste preferences, competitive promotions or other market dynamics there are still only three ways to drive food and beverage sales:

- Increase Reach (new customers)
- Increase Frequency (existing customer more often)
- Increase Check Average (sell the existing customer more)

While we cannot control the dynamics of changing consumer taste on maximizing the activities we can control. Raising prices to cover revenue targets is short lived and will never be a sustainable strategy.

Depending on budget, timing and desire for real change and long term sustainable results or desire for short term, topline sales, it will help dictate our response. If you can't write your strategy on the back of a bar napkin, it is too difficult.

It doesn't make a difference if it is a martial arts technique or a business strategy. Simplicity is everything. That is the reason high performing organizations only assign three or four business objectives to an individual or business unit. Most people cannot effectively focus or manage multiple things well. That is why whether you are a manager or an individual contributor, we only look to steward a handful of key business indicators. There are always a multitude of things employees can be doing in your business, however there are only a handful of things which actually drive your business. That is where you must place the organization's focus. We must learn to help others focus and separate activity from productivity.

It starts with clarity of vision, multiplication through inspiration, simplicity in execution and lastly ongoing rejuvenation which provides balance in both home and work. "Inside the Bubble" represents a compilation of events and behaviors that have influenced my successes in life and are designed to educate, motivate and empower entrepreneurs, existing leaders and inspiring leaders to live a value-driven life and help readers achieve growth through focus and balance.

It is not a book on protective services, but a narrative on business and leadership. The book contains a collection of *sixisms* (quotable phrases and metaphors), as well as business examples and considerations designed to inspire you to live your own value driven life.

"Vision always precedes inspiration. Thus vision is the only real superpower."

Chapter 1

Six on Business

Moving the Board

It is often said that sound business practices are like chess, not checkers. However, effective business strategy is not about moving the pieces, it's about moving the board!

Six on Business

One of the most important considerations I often share with people desiring to enter into the protective services industry is understanding the fundamental concept of risk mitigation versus risk management. One involves strategy. The other involves tactics.

I regularly get police officers, bodyguards and private citizens who ask me, "What do I do if someone grabs my gun?" Well if they understand the concept of proximity and maintain an appropriate distance away from a potential adversary, then they don't have to deal with "Plan B." While you may have the ability to manage within the crisis, if you can avoid it all together, that represents a much more efficient and effective strategy.

To quote Sun Tzu, "To fight and conquer in all our battles is not supreme excellence; supreme excellence consists in breaking the enemy's resistance without fighting."

Well, in general business before you can ever move forward, you must first understand exactly where you are today before you can attempt to develop a strategy to improve that positioning. Our SWOT analysis is the beginning of the organization of the strategy.

Six on Business

SWOT Analysis

People are often compelled to believe their businesses are so different from others. From this point forward, sever the notion that your business is so different and embrace the concept that while your business may be done across a different vertical segment, sound business practices are sound business practices regardless of industry. The same performance analysis tools employed by traditional businesses are the same types of analysis tools employed across a multitude of industries.

One commonly used tool to analyze a business, the market and the competitive landscape is the SWOT analysis (strengths, weakness opportunities, and threats). This tool serves the exact same purpose in traditional businesses as the risk analysis and threat assessment does in protective services. Both help you proactively assess the market or environment to mitigate risk or enhance your opportunity for success. Before you can be successful in moving the board, you have to first establish a method of objectively assessing where you are to determine your current positioning.

Strengths

What advantages does your organization have relative to the customer or market you desire to serve? What do you do better than anyone else? What is unique about your value proposition relative to your people, processes, goods or services?

It is only a strength if it directly impacts the needs of the customer or

Six on Business

consumer. It is only a unique strength if you are the only ones who can do it or can do it to a degree significantly greater than other competitors in the marketplace. Always calibrate your strengths against their relevance to the needs of your customer or consumer not your competitor. The more uniqueness you deliver relative to the needs of the customer, the less the customer's business decision will hinge on price or relationship.

Weaknesses

What are your product or service voids relative to the needs of the customer, consumer or market? Do you have gaps in market intelligence, consumer or customer experiences, geographic coverage, service or product alignment, price or technology? It is not a weakness if your competitor can do something and you cannot, if that competitors service has no bearing on the client's needs or desires. Having weaknesses doesn't mean you won't necessarily pursue a particular client or market, it just helps you understand where the challenges my come from.

Analyzing your weakness is an all guns on the table type of assessment. It is only through candid assessment can we make the best decisions to engage or withdraw.

Opportunities

Where is the market place heading? What are the current trends in your industry? Where will the new growth come from? Are there any changes in government regulations, technology or societal trends such as consumer

Six on Business

taste preferences, crime, or market growth?

Threats

What are your biggest impediments to growth? Are there any proposed changes in government regulations that may adversely impact your business? What role if any does technology have on your ability to impact the marketplace? Are there any new competitors in the marketplace that represent either a significant price or service advantage offering?

Your ability to candidly assess your market is critical to your success. It provides you the ability to maximize your value proposition, maintain your profits and drive long term sustainable growth and market share. It is okay to win slowly. It is okay to win fast. It is okay to lose fast, however what you want to truly avoid is losing slow as it represents a tremendous drain on organizational resources.

Learning to analyze your true points of differentiation allows you to pursue business on your terms and develop a value proposition relative to the needs of your customer, consumer or the market you desire to serve. Once you have done that you are now ready to establish your standards and benchmarks or aspirational objectives.

Six on Business

McDonalds never worried about where Burger King or Wendy's was considering building a restaurant. They researched the marketplace determined the growth opportunities and defined the fast food corridor, thereby receiving discounted real estate pricing, optimum street side positioning and preferred curb cuts on the highway.

Six on Business

Standards and Benchmarks

Every time, I get ready for work, I realize I am not only representing my clients, I am representing myself and my agency. Standards are benchmarks designed to hold you accountable. I will never have a client who demands more of me and my agency than we demand of ourselves.

Standards are benchmarks designed to hold you accountable. They are our mile markers in the road of life. They guide you in your actions and define acceptable behavior for yourself, your organization, your team or your family. They are the commitment to quality, your promise to deliver, or the expectations you set for your family. Without standards, you have no way of evaluating your performance. You can never achieve excellence if you don't first establish a baseline then determine your aspirational objectives. In business, if you don't first establish a standard, there is no way you can ever achieve excellence.

With time effectively done, your standards should become a point of differentiation in your service model. I remember when I considered taking an evasive and protective driving course; I started researching companies for possible consideration. Most companies didn't have any standards, at the end of the course all participants received a certificate of attendance. I then asked, "Well how do you calibrate success or improvement?" Most said you can just tell.

Six on Business

Then I followed up with the staff at the prestigious Tony Scotti Vehicle Dynamic Institute, and asked the same questions. They said we don't issue certificates of attendance. We issue credentials based on student performance. Our passing rate is based on the student's ability to be able to effectively utilize 80% of the vehicle's operating capability. Then I asked if they could put that in perspective for me.

"The average driver will never be able to effectively utilize more than 40% of the operating capabilities of their vehicle. A police driving instructor will typically utilize appropriately 55% of the capabilities of the vehicle. At Tony Scotti's VDI, unless a student can effectively utilize at least 80% of the capabilities of the vehicle they can't go on to the next exercise." Their goal is to objectively be able to help their students not only measure their improvement, but most importantly enhance their safety through quantifiable measurements.

That is an effective use of standards as a point of differentiation in their service model.

Six on Business

Brand Positioning

Positioning it is what your brand wants to be when it grows up.

Now that you have done your SWOT analysis and established your aspirational objectives, it is now time to put laser focus on the creation of your brand positioning statement which is often referred to as your brand strategy. Contrary to popular belief, branding is not about fancy slogans and tag lines. It's about focus, direction, consumers and creating emotional attachment. You can't begin to develop strategy, market, do PR or even effectively communicate to

Six on Business

your team until you first formulate your brand positioning statement.

The positioning statement is an internal communication tool designed to provide clear focus throughout your organization. It is not your marketing plan; it is the DNA from which your plan will be born.

Positioning Statement Format

To: _____ (Core user)

Brand X is the: _____ (Frame of reference)

That: _____ (Brand Benefits/Point of Differentiation)

Whether you are a consumer brand, political candidate, small business or a not-for-profit, your success or failure is dependent on your positioning!

Core user – the attitudinal and demographic description of the core prospect to whom the brand is intended to appeal to; this subset of customers are the most fervent users of your product or service.

Frame of Reference – the category in which the brand competes; the context that gives the brand relevance to the core user.

Brand Benefits/Point of Differentiation – the most compelling and motivating benefit that the brand can own in the hearts and minds of its target audience *relative* to the competition. This is what helps establish your emotional connection.

Let's look at brand power in action – King Louis

Louis Vuitton continues to position itself as timeless and authentic. It has been the most successful global luxury brand over the past five years.

Laser focus on its heritage as a travel brand helped it to retain its core customer – the jet setter. The brand invested in creativity, heightened its focus on quality and even increased its prices rather than compromising its brand value during the recession.

Revenues went up 4% to 29.1 billion euros.
Profits from recurring operations up 2% 6.01 billion euros[1].

Characteristics of High Performing Brands

Global luxury brands share many similar traits of prestige and exclusivity. Yet, each brand has its own identity and a distinct strategy of brand positioning that sets itself apart.

The most resilient luxury brands, like the best protection agencies increase brand value despite economic downturns. They focus on heritage and history instead of high fashion. Moreover, true luxury

---

[1] LVMH 2013 investor relations report January 30, 2014

Six on Business

companies show deliberate business consideration and do not relent on price or brand control.

They control every single component of their business model, from retail distribution to discounting. You must do the same with your image, that of your company or non-profit.

They established a compelling brand position/distinction over time that is meaningful, connected with consumers, which allowed them to leverage their value and innovate to keep them successful.

Brand Nike, as an example, changes approximately 30% of their product line every quarter primarily changing colors on their shoes and apparel every month. This allows them to maintain an advantage over their competitors and gives consumers a new reason to come back to retail.

Why is brand positioning so important?

Positioning is the key to communicating with your customers, clients, peers or employees.

Well-positioned brands send out a clear, consistent message which differentiates their brand from competitors or clearly describes who they are. It provides a clear vision of a brand's value to customers or consumers.

Poorly positioned brands often send out mixed messages and confuse their customers, clients, peers or employees.

Brand positioning helps your internal team understand how to focus and increase your organization's value proposition.

Six on Business

Brand Synergy

All the key elements of a successful brand work together.

Positioning is the heartbeat of every successful company or brand. Everything else your organization does revolves around it.

- Name
- Formula
- Packaging
- Pricing
- Advertising
- Distribution Channels
- Consumer Promotions
- Trade Promotion
- Publicity

Six on Business

Understanding Brand Oakley

Let's look at brand Oakley and see how all the positioning elements come together. Brand Oakley is positioned as a premier, authentic global performance brand.

Their *formula* is to pit the everyday hero against catastrophic odds at the ends of the world through cinematic brand alignment. We have seen them successfully execute this strategy with Christian Bale in the Terminator – Salvation as John Connor where he is featured in his Oakley's S.I Assault Boots. Matt Damon as Chief Warrant Officer Roy Miller in The Green Zone, and Denzel Washington with his Oakley Inmate Sunglasses and backpack in the Book of Eli.

Their *packaging* is simple, clean, aesthetically pleasing yet functional. They are *premium priced* and effectively manage their overstocks through their Oakley Vault (outlet) stores. Their *advertising* features athletes, soldiers, PSD operators, and other professionals using the product for its intended use, typically under adverse conditions.

In addition to their company stores, their *distribution channels*, represent high-end boutique and specialty shops consistent with their positioning of a premium priced brand.

They also maintain consumer relevance with *consumer promotions* via Facebook and Twitter. As for trade promotion, they offer professional use discounts for law enforcement, soldiers, overseas operators, professional athletes. Again, you see people using the

Six on Business

products for their intended use thereby reinforcing the authenticity of the brand.

During the Chilean miner rescue operation Oakley executed on one of the most successful *public relations* campaigns of all time. After the Chilean miners had been trapped underground for 69 days Oakley donated 35 pairs of black with iridium Radar wrap around sunglass to protect the miner's eyes during and post rescue. The product retail cost represented approximately $6,300[2]. Oakley received $41 million in equivalent advertising time exposure[3]. You can't even get a better return on that investment in Las Vegas.

How are you integrating all of the positioning elements as it relates to your brand to drive brand synergy, clarity of message and emotional connection with your targeted consumer?

---

[2] Oakley Chilean Miner Rescue Operation, October 13, 2010.

[3] CNBC – Oakley Gets projected $41 million in Exposure from Chilean Miners, October 13, 2010.

Six on Business

Driven to Please

Once you have established your standards, identified your points of differentiation and established your brand positioning, you must be driven to please. Developing a client centric culture first starts with a clear understanding of the customer you want to service. The entire organization has to believe that customers are their lifeblood. They are the reason we exist. Without satisfied customers, we have no need for products, services or employees.

Then, make sure everything from the services you offer, to the training you provide to your team, to your infrastructure, management controls, to your compensation plans all are aligned to help you serve your customer better. You have to develop a support culture that says, if you aren't directly serving a customer, you better be serving someone who is. Then you have to create culture where

16

Six on Business

people inspire to continue to get better. Source winners you need people who expect success and have the discipline to see it through.

Entrepreneurial Success

One of the most important keys to success is making your business scalable. Hire people who are functionally excellent in the various sectors of your business and allow them to cross train others, then diversify your revenue streams to allow you to survive volatility in the marketplace. Even as you diversify your revenues streams there should be an integration in the services so they complement your overall positioning.

Below are the Top 6 characteristics I believe every entrepreneur should have.

- *Competency in your trade* – this is not an option it represents the minimal point of entry. Those skills must be defined by some level of differentiation to provide you a competitive edge in the marketplace.
- *Passion* – you need something that drives you beyond money because in the early days making significant returns may be a rare commodity. Also, once you start making money if you don't maintain that passion for excellence the first casualty of success is often quality control or service.
- Spirit of Service – you must be compelled to deliver a phenomenal customer experience every time.
- *Capital* (most businesses fail because they are undercapitalized) – build your business Performa on the worst

Six on Business

case scenario. Then understand you will probably still be more optimistic than your executional or business development capabilities manifest themselves.

- *Stamina* – initially the hours will be long. You must have the physical, mental and emotional capacity to stay the course.
- *Task Switching* – understand the importance and difference of task switching versus multi-tasking. Multi-tasking is the path to mediocrity. When you multi-task you don't do anything well. When you task switch it provides laser focus to each critical activity. You learn to complete critical tasks sequentially versus simultaneously doing nothing well.

My humble advice is follow your passion and the money will always catch up. Most long term successful careers and businesses are built on personal strengths used by people who enjoy what they do. Mark Cuban owner of the Dallas Mavericks says, "Don't start a company unless it's an obsession and something you love. If you have an exit strategy it's not an obsession."[4] However, don't confuse enthusiasm with competency and business development.

Don't step out on your own until you have clearly identified your point of difference in the marketplace and have the capital to execute on that vision.

---

[4] Mark Cuban 12 Rules for Start Ups, January 10, 2012.

Six on Business

Mark Cuban, "If you have an exit strategy it's not an obsession."

Six on Business

The Uh Huh Moment

That critical moment when the entrepreneur realizes their success is a combination of trade skill coupled with business acumen. Until that point, it is called a hobby.

Six on Business

Your best advertisement will always be your work. The best client you have is the one you currently have. For most businesses, a large concentration of their business comes from referrals. Also, 5% of your clients will typically give you 50% of your revenue. Protecting that 5% and having the infrastructure to support them is critical to maintaining that business relationship.

That infrastructure must manifest itself in both strategic technical/operational integration and relationship alignment both high and wide. You must add value at both the executive and operational level. Too often, we see organizations focus on one at the exclusion of the others. If all of your focus is on signing the initial contract via the executive level and you don't maintain connection with the operational levels of the client's organization, you will reduce the opportunity to ensure your organization is delivering value on a daily basis. Remember when something is not working or our clients experience a service level failure, it is the operational level who feels the pain first.

Conversely, if all you focus on is the operational level and you don't effectively communicate the return on investment the client is receiving or will receive at the executive level, you reduce your ability to secure the initial funding or to be treated like a commodity on a go forward basis, being relegated to a purchasing department request for pricing (RFP) or bid.

Six on Business

Leveraging Success

Learn to leverage the relationships of your existing clientele. Birds of a feather often flock together. The best time to secure future business is when your existing customers are already satisfied with your services and performance. Also showcase your thought leadership via public relations, your website, your publications, social media and speaking engagements. Strategic partnerships with complementary businesses can also help drive incremental growth.

Make your vision transparent and simplify your execution. That starts with your brand positioning and organizational ventriloquism. Your team has to be unified in voice, vision and execution. You must establish very clear brand positioning so everyone on your staff understands who they are, what they are and how they deliver value. That vision should also be very clear to your customer, so they recognize you when they need you.

Six on Business

Building a Winning Team

The key to building a high performing team is to surround yourself with like-minded people who have diverse skills and are focused on a common objective.

Once you have established your points of differentiation and your brand strategy, it is now time to select the team that will help you execute on that service model. Once you have determined technical competency, one of the critical traits I look for in sourcing/recruiting

Six on Business

talent is a winning disposition. I don't care if the winning has come from a prior sports life, business or a dog competition. With winners typically comes discipline. Otherwise, the individual would not have had the ability to consistently perform at a high level.

If an individual has discipline, he or she possesses the ability and dedication to build the required skills that help enhance their personal development and overall team competencies. You can teach skills. You can't teach traits.

While a great management practice is recognizing and rewarding positive performance and I support that practice, I am driven to people who take initiative as it is one of the fundamental underpinnings of leadership. With self-starters you don't have to send a parade to their home or office in order for them to be motivated toward performance.

I also look for positive people with a team orientation, for that fosters camaraderie and healthy competition. The last critical competency I look for is a demonstrated ability to successfully manage through adversity. Despite how successful an organization or individual may become, I like someone who has had to manage through an adverse situation in their life, whether business or personal. For if there are any setbacks, there won't be complete devastation and they typically have a built in level of resilience.

Six on Business

Competency is defined as demonstrated capability.
Never confuse enthusiasm
with competency!

Six on Business

People often confuse training with skill attainment. Training exposes you to concepts. However, only practice can build skills. For most people, training is an event. There is generally not enough repetition built into the exercises to truly develop the skill.

While most attendees share excitement when they return home from a training event, unless you build the skill development into their standard operating procedures to allow them to reinforce the training, you cannot expect a return on your initial training activity or event.

If you are not going to commit to the reinforcement, don't waste the money on the initial training. Spend the money on a corporate or company boondoggle, they will have fun, some may bond but neither has an expectation for learning or knowledge transfer.

Some may think that if a person can do the activity 85% of the time, it is considered a skill. If the person packing my parachute only did it correctly 85% of the time, I would truly hate to be part of that unfortunate 15%. It is only a skill if you can consistently do it on demand.

Six on Business

Business Demand Driven Training

Training should always be business demand driven.

Keep your training business demand driven. We don't train to train, we train to assist in the accomplishment of our business objectives. The top performing companies never stop training and it is always strategically integrated into the larger plan, as they are always looking for additional ways to sharpen the saw, create or maintain a point of difference in the marketplace or increase the morale of the team.

Six on Business

When you contrast that with the notion of mid-tier or low performing organizations during financially challenged times, the training budgets are often one of the first budgets to get cut because they are just viewed as expense items. Despite what most organizations may think, this is the time when you must maintain organizational discipline and stay the course.

As a former business consultant who focused on performance development, below is a series of questions I typically asked my clients every year as we prepared to address their upcoming objectives.

1. What are your top three objectives for the upcoming year or 18 months?

2. What are your strategies to accomplish those objectives?

3. What do you see as the biggest impediments or challenges to accomplishing those objectives?

4. What are the skills required of the team to accomplish those objectives?

5. When you look at the skills that are tied to objectives one, two or three, what percentage of your revenue plan is tied to each of those objectives?

6. Which skills does the team have today and which ones still need to be enhanced or developed?

Six on Business

For ease of discussion, let's say 15% of your revenue plan is tied to client retention, and 10% is tied to new product or service line extension and both are areas that need to be developed. If we are not prepared to enhance their client retention development then we have the potential to miss our revenue plan by 15%. So if you are not going to train the team on how to enhance that skill, where are you going to pick up the incremental 15% revenue as we just acknowledged the team didn't have those competencies? Same question goes for the service line extension objectives.

Thus, we don't merely train to train. We train to accomplish our business objectives. By keeping your training business demand driven, you will never have a problem securing training budget because the training budget is written into the operating plan as it is an integral part of the overall revenue generation or client retention strategy.

Six on Business

Understanding Sales and Marketing

Understand the difference between sales and marketing and the impact of both.

Once you have established your positioning and developed your service model it is now time to start communicating with the marketplace. Marketing is a process of communicating the value of your product or services to your customers or consumers with the expressed purpose of selling more. Marketing is not about creating programs, it is about creating consumer connections, which manifest themselves into sales. If your marketing team's performance

Six on Business

objectives and compensation plans are not about helping the organization gain new clients or sell more products and services, then they are focused on the wrong objectives.

Marketing is about communicating one to many, whereas sales is about communicating one to one. Good marketing programs both educate and motivate customers or consumers to take action. Effective marketing provides warm leads for those tasked with business development or sales.

Cut Through the Clutter

Six on Business

Weapons don't make you a better warrior they just extend your reach, just as marketing doesn't make you a better company, it just elevates your voice.

A loud voice without clarity and focus creates distortion. So before you develop and communicate a robust marketing plan, make sure you have the infrastructure to support it, in addition to the execution capabilities to handle the anticipated increase in traffic.

Creating customer or consumer excitement and then not being able to execute on fulfillment is just paying your customers to go to your competitor.

Understanding Sales

Sales are transactions between two parties, wherein one party (the buyer) receives goods or services in exchange for money. Until the exchange of compensation occurs, it is just distribution. Whether you are a large corporation, entrepreneur or non-profit, sales (revenue generation or funding) is king. It is not queen, prince, princess or court jester. Outside of revenue generation everything else is just a cost center. While the other business units or departments may be very important cost centers, no organization can survive without ongoing revenue, or a funding source in the case for non-profits. So an organization's most important task is ongoing revenue generation or business development.

Six on Business

Contrary to what some will have you believe there is no such thing as a person with a gift for gab, so abandon that mindset immediately. No one wants to be sold, hounded, harassed or pestered. People want to feel like they are making intelligent buying decisions. You don't waste your time trying to convenience people to buy. People only buy when they have a need. They have to be motivated to see a change in their current situation. Your organization's job, therefore, is to find those clients who are motivated to do different now versus later. That shortens the sales cycle. That is the only time a customer or consumer is ready to take action.

Until a customer sees a perceived need, your job is not to sell, but merely to educate and keep your company top of mind so when they are motivated you are the company they contact.

Always remember in consumer products, the *sell through* will always be more important than the *sell in*. The *sell in* is usually a test of your initial credibility. The *sell through* is what creates repeat sales and is the foundation of the ongoing business relationship. Helping your clients stream line their efficiencies, enhance their revenues, extend their capabilities or help them navigate safely is your primary focus. In the service industry, it is truly performing as advertised. Very rarely will you and your client differ on your objectives. However, from time to time you may differ on strategy.

I remember during my time as a regional manager with a major athletic vendor while working with one of our large regional sports retailers, who was desiring to further enhance his revenues. Their strategy for growth and enhancement was to ask for larger quantities

Six on Business

of a vastly allocated, high margin and high dollar item products. As a wholesaler our strategy was to keep the product limited in the marketplace which is what allows it to maintain both its high margins and retail ticket price.

When we started discussing how much potential additional profit would be generated, we determined the increased profit would represent approximately $700,000. I then confirmed their objective was to generate an incremental $700,000. I asked if we could show him how to do that and more, would he be interested. He said absolutely.

I then asked three questions. First, approximately what percentage of their customers were male? The answer, 85%. We then confirmed on average we were selling the male consumer approximately five to six pairs of athletic shoes and items of apparel per year. Second question asked was approximately how many pairs of shoes and items of apparel are you selling to women annually? The answer, approximately two. Final question was what do you think realistically are the chances of selling the men two to three incremental pair of athletic shoes per year? The retailer said it will take some work or added incentive (that is code name for sale). As a premium brand, the word "sale" is a word to avoid, as it often equates to lost margin and brand devaluation.

Since the retail owner and I were approximately the same age, I knew much of his point of reference around females playing sports was potentially dated. I informed him that when he and I were in high school one in twenty five girls played a sport and that today it was one in four. If he wanted to increase his chances of significantly selling more shoes and apparel annually, he needed to expand his thinking of incremental market penetration. Also developing an enhanced women's focus would give him additional differentiation in the marketplace.

We then decided to help the team visualize the creation of a women's sports destination via enhanced retailer theater at one of their high profile Washington, DC stores. We also shared with them the information gained through our female focus groups about how they desired to be serviced while shopping. One of the critical things the focus groups revealed was that women don't want to feel pressured when shopping. We encouraged them to modify the interior design of the store, slightly lowering the profile softening the image to give a woman the impression of shopping in her living room. Who said function couldn't be aesthetically pleasing? Next, we co-opted some in-store appearances with one of our local WNBA athletes and branded the imaging on the outer wall of the two story building. This further established their commitment to the female athlete and stimulated many of the local WNBA fans to visit the store and further established their commitment to this consumer. Needless to say the program generated five times his originally projected incremental revenue and profit targets.

When you focus on the customer, consumer value and helping your clients drive topline sales, the discussion often shifts from cost to value. Discounting your products or services will never make you a better option, it just makes you a cheaper option and less profitable as a company. Until you learn to understand the impact of your products and services on your client's business, you will never really learn how to communicate your value. Most of the time the cost of your products and services only represent between 5 – 15% of the revenue you often help your customers generate. The best sales or business development people don't sell anything. They just help both parties come to an agreement on terms and find mutually beneficial ways to accomplish the joint objectives.

Discounting your products or services doesn't make you a better option, it just makes you a cheaper option and less profitable as a company.

Six on Business

Enhancing Communication

Speak less, listen more.

Effective communication can only be achieved through active listening. Learn to speak less and listen more. Attorneys are taught to never ask a question they feel they don't already know the answer to. While it may be an effective strategy in the courtroom, it has the complete opposite effect on enhancing real learning in business or life.

Six on Business

If we truly seek to understand, we must be prepared to ask questions we don't already know the answer to. Including the ones that make us uncomfortable. One of the best ways to demonstrate active listening is by taking notes, or paraphrasing the other person's communication points. Active listening is one of the most critical tools in developing the client's needs analysis. We can never bring about the best solution or a lasting resolution if we are afraid of hearing or understanding the actual problem or challenge.

Six on Business

Managing Group Interaction

Managing group meetings can be like herding cats.

The best way to strategically manage the discussion is not by talking more, but learning to manage the agenda. The person who is actually in charge or control is the one who is asking the questions or controlling the agenda.

Avoid conducting a group meeting without developing and circulating the objectives/purpose, as well as the tentative agenda. Very rarely do people disagree on the objectives although we often may disagree on the strategy.

Six on Business

Learn to pre-sell the agenda in advance particularly with the key stakeholders or group powerbrokers. This allows you to gain early support or at least anticipate where the greatest challenges will come during the discussion.

The agenda is a non-judgmental way to professionally manage the topic, energy and pace of the meeting. It also allows you to effectively manage surprise visitors or detractors, by allowing you to circle back to the meeting's purpose and larger goal as the framework to provide structure and discipline to the meeting or discussions.

Utilizing future meetings or the virtual parking lot (separate flipchart for items to be addressed later) allows the meeting to stay on track and maintain the positive momentum on the agreed upon items.

Six on Business

"Is there an app for that?"

Six on Business

The benefits of apps for business are numerous. First they allow your customers to work the way they live. They significantly enhance interaction by allowing your customers, consumers or employees to interface with your organization 24/7/365 at their convenience. A smartly designed app can be ongoing advertising for your business keeping you top of mind. They make business communication more efficient and appealing particularly when the apps are designed to interface with smart-devices. With over 120 million smart phone devices in the marketplace you are actually conspicuous by your absence if you are not taking advantage of that consumer interface.

Customer loyalty is also established through app development as people find it easier to access relevant information to make better buying decisions. In addition to the promotional aspects of the business, subscription based apps also provide a secondary source of revenue generation.

For customer facing organizations the real time data capture puts the information in the hands of those closest to your customer sales force. It also allows management an efficient way to leverage best practices or contingency plans more quickly to address shortfalls or negative variances.

Embrace technology, but don't become a slave to it. I have never met a technology department within a major corporation that was not incredibly busy and also never found a project they didn't think they could do better themselves as opposed to purchasing technology. So there is always the pressure of "make versus buy" when it comes to technology enhancing improvements. Also countless dollars have

Six on Business

been wasted on customer relationship management systems by CFOs and CIOs in an effort to monitor organizational performance or maintain a span of control. Remember a CRM system doesn't make you better it just helps you keep score and share information over space quicker.

So whether you are purchasing a CRM system or downloading an application if it does not allow your customer facing teams to first serve your customers better, you have the wrong approach.

Process empowers productivity, technology empowers process. Put technology on a bad process and you just do bad things faster. So, before you can automate a process you must first understand and refine it. Also, don't make your process adhere to technology make technology support your client engagement process.

For small businesses with growth of the major data warehouses, the large company functionality has never been easier via Cloud – Analytics – Mobile – Social – Security (C.A.M.S.S.). Cloud technology allows you to maintain the cutting edge information technology without the capital intensive hardware infrastructure investments. Cloud computing allows you to address two of the greatest challenges often plaguing information departments increasing capacity or adding capabilities. It generally affords you minimal additional training or new software licensing.

Six on Business

In its narrowest interpretation, Cloud is often referred to as virtual servers available over the Internet. However, in reality anything you consume outside of your firewall is "in the cloud."

The analytic capture capabilities allows your marketing department to collect feedback and data about your customer's behavior, location, preferences, spending habits and limits allowing your organization to better tailor consumer specific products, programs or services.

The mobile functionality eliminates or significantly reduces the need for costly catalogs, binders and other paper related costs. The enhanced portability of the smart phone versus personal computer is also preferred by both consumers and sales forces.

The social media exchange is also greatly enhanced via smart apps as there is no better advertisement than word of mouth. Effective interaction via social media also helps eliminate the wasted postage costs of direct mail campaigns and can efficiently target your desired consumer via more focused adverting campaigns.

Similarly, with the utilization of the major data warehouses to secure your data, you often enhance the safeguarding of your data from both breach, system outages and failures, fire and further reduce your liability or develop a more effective shared risk model. Whenever possible, consider an encrypted cloud service provider.

Six on Business

Long-term Sustainable Results

Long-term, sustainable results can never be achieved through random acts of brilliance. They can only be achieved through an ongoing commitment to excellence and standardizing success.

Six on Business

If you look at the best performing organizations, whether they are business organizations, sports teams or high performing military units, they all have found ways to standardize success. Whether it is a corporate bench strength program, sports farm system, induced stress to consistent repetition of a military unit to engrain muscle memory.

No organization can experience long-term sustainable results through random acts of brilliance. That can only be achieved through ongoing consistent performance.

High performing organizations constantly share best practices. What separates the top 5% from the top 25% is consistency. Both do great things, the top 5% just do them more frequently. When you share and standardize best practices you allow the top 25% to perform at a higher level (often like a five or ten percenter).

Because of their competitive, drive the top 5% will continue to charge harder and work even smarter as they enjoy being high performers. So, high tide floats all boats and success becomes contagious.

As a sales leader and performance consultant one of the most impactful ways I was able help standardize the success of my teams and that of my clients, along with significantly enhancing the teams' on-call execution was to shift the focus from call reporting to call planning. Once a sales person makes a call they either accomplished their sales call objective or they didn't. Post call there is little impact a sales peer or supervisor could have on that call, and once a clients has said, no the cost of re-engagement is always significantly higher.

Six on Business

When I looked at the preparation process for top performers. They all did a significant amount of research and preparation in advance of trying to secure the appointment. That helped them to develop compelling business reasons which tied back to their client's key business drivers which helped them secure the meetings. Then on call they stewarded all of the discussions of their features, advantages and benefits back to that particular customer/buyer's measure of currency whether it was return on investment, operational efficiency, revenues or cost savings.

Your clients receive value from activating your services, so when you help your clients accomplish their objectives, funding your sales initiatives becomes a mandatory byproduct.

Six on Business

The Last Line of Defense

Always avoid being the first and last line of defense.

When I was younger in my business career, I had a great district manager who I thought walked on water. He was a great mentor, motivator and a hell of a closer (he could make a deal happen). Everyone in the district always wanted him on a sales call because we knew the deal would get done.

As I advanced from sales manager, to district manager, to regional manager and eventually to senior vice president of sales and marketing, I started to see that the biggest critical factor in the decision making process was access to information. If a person has a certain amount of intellectual capital and you give them sales

Six on Business

manager information and focus, they will make sales manager decisions (monthly/quarterly/annual plan). If you give them vice president information and responsibilities (semi-annual, annual, three year operating plan) they will make vice president types of decisions.

We teach young sales people to "sell high." That means get to the highest level decision maker you can in the buying organization. They get there and then what? While deferring to a higher authority is a negotiating tactic, it does not accelerate sales performance. I later realized the reason my former district manager was so good. He was empowered to say "yes." Sales representatives were not.

So while every day you watch sales people get to the appropriate level in the buying organization, unless you empower them with the ability to say yes, by default you are slowing the sale process down.

By giving your people parameters in which to negotiate and operate, and giving them the authority to say yes, you enhance client satisfaction, empower your people and accelerate the sales cycle or business development process.

Six on Business

Articulating Your Value

Never allow someone else to determine your value; you may not like the exchange rate.

You must learn how to articulate the value of your services. That is why ongoing business reviews are important. At minimum, make sure you are doing informal quarterly reviews and formal reviews semi-annually or annually.

The biggest challenge for many service providers is they don't establish measurable performance behaviors on the front end, so they have nothing to steward in order to manage ongoing performance.

Thus, by default you have now allowed others to subjectively define your value.

An established review process allows you to professionally take credit, for the value you add. In economically challenged times, accountants and business managers often look to high dollar line items to make cost reductions. If you are waiting for the expense reduction discussion to communicate your value, you are already too late, as others have now reconciled their decisions and are now looking for confirmation.

Most corporations or high net worth individuals don't have budget issues, they have revenue generation, safety or brand protection issues, so you must efficiently steward the discussions in the appropriate revenue, safety, brand protection context or whatever else may be their measure of currency.

Don't Front Money for Millionaires

It is amazing how those who have acquired the most are often the first to ask for yours. Don't front money for millionaires. This is a principle I subscribed to in my prior life as a corporate executive and continue today as an entrepreneur.

Large corporations are notorious for asking vendors to agree to extended terms as it is a way for them to get value from your services before they have to pay the invoice or as a way of managing the interest on their money over a longer period of time. For small

Six on Business

businesses one of the biggest challenges they face is managing cash flow so extended terms can literally be a killer.

Most financially independent people have acquired their wealth on the concept of OPE or OPM.

- Other people's efforts, or
- Other people's money.

You should seek to avoid allowing people to take advantage of your services or discount your value. You must learn to communicate how your value helps extend their service offering, personal safety or brand value.

I remember meeting with the representatives of a NBA player about providing protective services for an event for the player's non-profit foundation. That night was going to be a who's who of the city's shakers and movers. The event was going to be held at a very nice hotel, open bar and sit down dinner. After explaining the tentative activities they asked if I would consider donating my services for the charitable event.

I smiled and asked, "How did you hear about my agency?" They said, "You came highly recommended by several players and local business people." I then went on to talk about some of the potential challenges of the evening they may face and asked them how were they prepared to handle them. They communicated they hadn't thought about said issues and had not developed any contingency plans for those circumstances if they arose.

Six on Business

I gave them some suggestions on how they could potentially be handled. They said, "Wow! Could you possibly handle those things and particularly those questions if they come up with the press?" I said we could.

We then got back to discussing the financial considerations for that event, I asked whether the hotel was donating the event space, the meals or the open bar. They said, "Why, no." I asked whether the hotels would be donating any free sleeping rooms for the out of town guests. They said, "No." I said, "Since your player was drafted has he ever played one minute in the NBA without being compensated?" They said, "Of course not. He worked really hard to develop his skills and command his salary." I let them know that I respected that viewpoint and felt the same way.

While we would have been happy to provide services for the event, we would not be in a position to do it without compensation or at a discount rate based on the high profile nature of the event and the appropriate risks associated with it. They agreed to pay our normal rates. The bottom line, pun intended, is if you can't find a way to communicate your value, you can't expect anyone else to respect it. Remember, a contract is only a contract if both parties agree.

Six on Business

Why Small Businesses Fail

Most small businesses fail not because the owners are not well intended or may not have good trade skills, but often because they are undercapitalized. So, before you put out your shingle make sure you have the reserves to invest in your future. You can't just build it and they will come, you have to also market it so they know you exist.

Six on Business

In the movie "300" there is a pivotal scene where King Leonidas meets Daxos and the other Arcadians as they prepare to go to war together against the Persian army. In the scene, Daxos looks at King Leonidas with some disappointment as he doesn't feel King Leonidas has brought enough soldiers to fight. King Leonidas then looks at Daxos' troops and asks the first gentleman, "What is your profession?"

The soldier replies, "Potter."

Leonidas turns to the next man and asks, "You?"

The soldier replies, "Sculptor."

Yet another soldier is asked, "You?"

That soldier replies, "Blacksmith."

King Leonidas then turns to his troops and roars, "Spartans, what is your profession?" The Spartans all bang their spears on the ground indicating we do just one thing, we are warriors.

If you want to have a successful business you must commit to being a Spartan. I regularly meet people who tell me they are a protection specialist and they hand me their business cards which read realtor, landscaper, painter and so on. They aren't protection specialists. They are the occupations on their cards. That is where they have invested their training.

Six on Business

Protective services is not a low cost of entry profession. I would also go on to say it is not just a profession it is a vocation. Like any other professional industry it requires planning, investments and ongoing development. To borrow a phrase from Las Vegas, "you got to be all in!" That doesn't say you should not diversify your revenue streams within the desired sector but you can't serve two masters and do it well. Take time. Build your skills across your desired spectrum.

If you are going to be a professional you have to act like one. You should be doing something in your profession every day. Professional athletes train five to six times per week, Doctors practice medicine every day, attorney's either research the law or litigate every day. Take that same commitment to your development. Build your skills and the money will come.

Chapter 2

Six on Leadership

*Experience always comes with scars. Wisdom is
not getting the same scar twice.*

Six on Leadership

Leading from the Front

Bend over and pick up that piece of paper.

First and foremost, leading is not about doing, but learning to become an enabler of doers and providing the inspiration and competency to help people succeed and perform in your absence. It is helping each and every employee understand when all else is equal the difference is ME (maximum effort).

One of my good friends is a general manager of a fine dining restaurant. He is the perfect embodiment of always *leading from the front*. At some point in his career, I have watched him perform every function in each of his restaurants. I have never once watched him walk past a piece of paper on the floor or not grabbing a mop to assist in cleaning up a spill, if he was close to an accident.

I use the paper on the floor as a metaphor for leading from the front. He has, through his actions, communicated to his staff that there will never be a reason for our restaurants to ever be untidy. If I won't walk past something out of place neither should you. As a leader, if you are too afraid to get your hands dirty, then I can never see your establishment as clean.

Six on Leadership

While we all have different primary functions based on our individual competencies and our daily operating responsibilities, we should never be too big to do a small task. Leadership – whether you are a sales leader, restaurant operator or tactical commander – is most effective when it comes from the front.

In the words of Edgar A. Guest, "I would rather see a good sermon than hear one."

Managing with Courage

Don't be afraid to manage with courage.

Six on Leadership

One of the clearest signs of a high performing organization is how it manages under-performance. Managing with courage does not mean managing by intimidation. It is managing with clarity, honesty and objectivity. The focus is on performance and performance enhancement, not personality.

Unlike antiquated management models wherein excessive amounts of time were placed with non-performers, today most high performing organizations represent up or out cultures. They place their focus and time with those who are having a positive impact on the business.

Best of breed find ways to trim the fat of underperforming employees. They focus on correcting *skill* issues, they don't waste time with *will* issues. Training fixes *skill* issues. Only honest, candid feedback and performance improvement plans can address *will* issues. The acid test is if I threatened you with severe bodily harm if you didn't perform the task and you can do it then it is not a skill issue. It is a will issue.

Now the question has to center on why the employee is not choosing to engage in the desired behavior. Sometimes good performance is punishing. Whenever I do a good job, you put more stuff on my plate, as opposed to addressing the underperformer which is causing a disproportionate distribution of work without additional compensation.

If underperformance is attributed to lack of skill, that is a training issue and we address that immediately, as the employee has the will and desire, they just don't have the requisite skill.

Six on Leadership

After the initial training is performed and we have an employee who previously added value, but just cannot step up to the new requirements of the job, we then look to identify where are their skills best utilized in the organization and focus on reassignment rather than outplacement.

If there is a reorganization or you are bringing in new management and you know there are current employees who need to be separated that process should take place with the prior manager or senior leader. Don't make a forced separation be the first act of the new leader. It is not that they don't have the ability to conduct the separation discussion. They often will not have witnessed the pinpointed, observable behaviors which were the root causes of the separation. Also, for the existing employees they have inherited, it will represent a time of uneasiness and potential discomfort as you will create a culture of compliance versus acceptance.

Managing with courage is the truest form of compassion as your goal is to help place the employee in a position where they can best add value consistent with their competencies and personal interest. For some, that may be outside of the company. If outplacement eventually becomes the best option, always do it with compassion. Always allow the individual to save face during the discussion and transition process. Whether that is reflected in their severance arrangement (compensation), access to outplacement services or leaving their voicemail on for an additional 30 days while they conduct their employment search, separation with respect should be your goal.

Six on Leadership

Don't tolerate negativity or insubordination.

Don't waste time with negativity or people who are not committed to the success of the business units or teams. Negativity drains the energy of the unit.

General Colin Powell in one of his books on leadership says, "I hate weak generals. They talk behind your back and undermine the success of mission or unit." They should be cut out like a cancer because if they will undermine the leader, they will undermine the team and ultimately the client.

As a leader we should encourage an open door policy and sharing a

Six on Leadership

point of view. Often the best solutions are often created by those closest to the customer or represent a hybrid of multiple considerations so never suppress feedback. As the business unit leader you still reserve the ability to say no and implement your individual strategy. That is the accountability that comes with the responsibility.

However never tolerate insubordination. And once the decision is made then we all must move in the consistent direction with no additional discussion outside of execution.

There can only be one vision because two visions equals division, and two heads is a monster.

Six on Leadership

It is not my place to tell another man how he should live his life. But, when another man's actions start to impact me and my family, it is time for us to have a discussion.

Six on Leadership

"For each will have to bear his own load."
Galatians 6:5

Whether you subscribe to the above biblical passage or *Michael Baisden's "Minding your business eliminates half the problems in your life,"* I think both represent sound advice and wisdom that we all should aspire to embrace.

Everything does not need to be your fight! One of the biggest signs of maturity is knowing when to get involved and when to say, "Not my issue." However, arrogance and entitlement sometimes override logic and common sense.

It will never be my place to tell another man how he should live his life. But, when another man's actions start to impact me and my family, it is time for us to have a discussion.

Six on Leadership

"Civilization depends on, and civility often requires, the willingness to say, 'What you are doing is none of my business' and 'What I am doing is none of your business."

George Will

Six on Leadership

Standing Alone

Standing alone doesn't mean you are not popular or don't have a lot of friends. It just means your friends are not required for you to have a point of view.

I realized a long time ago the reason it is called self-esteem is it does not require anyone's permission but yours. The sooner you realize that, the happier you will be!

While I sometimes may be the only one who shares a point of view, it doesn't mean that I stand alone. For I stand on strong shoulders. I

Six on Leadership

come from a legacy of strong men and women, born of principle and character. They survived the Middle Passage, the Peculiar Institution, the Removal Act, the death camps of Auschwitz, apartheid and every other atrocity known to man.

For I would insult their legacy if I did not stand up for my point of view as they shed their blood, sweat and tears to give me the right to take that stand.

Standing alone does not mean you are not approachable, it just means in the final analysis, you have chosen to take a different position. That is the accountability that goes with the responsibility of being the team lead or business unit leader. Sometimes it can be the result of sensitive information which may not be privy to the rest of the team at the required time of action. As a professional we are often tasked with learning to separate being friendly from being friends.

However, remember a good leader shares the sunshine but stands in the rain alone.

Six on Leadership

Effective Delegation

Delegation is designed to extend the capabilities of the team, not make the leader's job easier. However, you cannot delegate to someone who doesn't have the competencies. Thus, your greatest responsibility as a leader is to develop your team.

Six on Leadership

Delegation (noun)

1. a group of people who are chosen to vote or act for someone else.
2. the act of giving control, authority, a job, a duty, etc., to another person.

Through the years delegation has been beat down, abused and spit on. Bottom line – delegation has gotten a bad rap based on rouge managers who have used it as a dumping ground, punishment or some other form of de-motivation.

Delegation is designed to extend the capabilities of the team or organization, not make the leader's job easier. It should be viewed as a vote of confidence in the individual assigned the task and an opportunity for growth and development. However, you cannot delegate something to someone who doesn't have the competencies. Thus, your greatest responsibility as a leader will always be the ongoing development of your team.

One of the most effective ways to utilize delegation is as a stretch objective and developmental training in a low risk initiative. It provides a development opportunity for the team member and extends the future capacity of the business unit.

Six on Leadership

Courtesy and Diplomacy

Of all the skills I have tried to master through the years, courtesy and diplomacy are our greatest assets.

When people often think about protective services, they often think about what is often referred to as the hard skills such as defensive tactics, firearms training, protective and evasive driving. The things we historically see in the movies like brass flying, ladies crying and, you know, bad guys dying. But unlike the latest James Bond or Jason Bourne movie we try to avoid the fanfare and leave the drama for

Six on Leadership

Hollywood.

Boring/uneventful days are our measures of success. If I can give my VIP client 45 extra minutes a day over the course of the week, I have given them almost a full working day of time back to themselves and their families. Our job is about facilitation. How can we make the situation better?

Through the years, the two skills I have relied on the most in order to efficiently do my job are courtesy and diplomacy. Kindness is contagious and most appreciated by all. Whether it's a contentious moment in a nightclub or an unanticipated interaction with customs abroad mutual respect is a language understood by all.

I treat every man and woman like they are the most important in the world, for at the moment in time they are. I was once told by one of my first mentors to never look down upon anyone, not even the man who shines my shoes. He also shines the CEO's shoes. Honesty, integrity and respect while take you around the world and with minimal adverse interaction. Because I love my culture it doesn't mean I don't RESPECT yours.

Six on Leadership

While all protectors and protectees desire to develop relationship chemistry, you must avoid becoming familiar for it breeds complacency. Always maintain the professionalism and never stop being your client's superhero.

Six on Leadership

While relationship chemistry is an aspiration of all protectors and protectees, you must avoid becoming complacent. The minute you become part of the entourage, is the minute the relationship is destine for failure. Our clients hire us for our skills not our friendship. If they can't trust us to maintain the integrity of our working relationship, how can they trust us with their lives?

In the business world while customer entertainment is often a standard part of enhancing the business relationship, we must continue to guard against becoming careless and always maintain the appropriate level of respect and deference in all of our business interactions. Never stop stewarding your client's key business indicators, because friendly clients may come and go, but the business drivers of their organization will remain fairly constant, thereby always allowing your company to stay contemporary.

"Professionalism is like love: it is made up of the constant flow of little bits of proof that testify to devotion and care. Everything else is pretension or incompetence."

- Tomislav Sola

Always maintain the professionalism, and never stop being your client's superhero. The moment you become Clark Kent, you can never go back to being Superman again.

Six on Leadership

Strategic Partnerships

Strategic partnerships help extend your capacity and capabilities while helping you enhance service delivery and elevate the standards of your industry.

Six on Leadership

The greatest competition you should ever face is when you look in the mirror. Your focus should be defined by your desire to serve your clients and enhance your industry.

Success is not a random act or something you can buy across the counter. You can't look it up in Google, you have to aspire to want to get better every day not merely by your words but by your actions. As a successful organization, you must learn how to make your actions scale. All successful organizations share best practices internally in an effort to enhance efficiency. The best organizations benchmark themselves against both people inside their industry, as well as outside of their industry. Best in breed is not always a function of existing pedigree, sometimes it is an entirely different breed.

Establishing strategic partnerships can help extend both your capabilities, overall capacity and provide you additional standards to help you and your organization calibrate its readiness and foster its ongoing development. Only iron can sharpen iron.

Six on Leadership

Never Underestimate

I promise, it won't work out like you think.

"I promise, it won't work out like you think," (accompanied by a smile). This is a phrase I have uttered from time to time in my career when I saw someone about to grossly under estimate the forthcoming sequence of events.

In the movie "The Book of Eli" with actor Denzel Washington, there is a pivotal scene in the movie where he is sitting at a bar and the local town bully starts to harass Denzel after he shoos a cat off the bar. He responds with, "It won't happen again, I promise. I don't want any trouble." The local bully answers, "That's too bad!" Denzel

Six on Leadership

regretfully is forced to open up an industrial strength can of whoop ass and defeats the local bully and his gang.

The moral of the story is never take kindness for weakness. Just because a man or woman doesn't want a confrontation, doesn't mean they are not prepared, capable or well skilled enough to have one. The quiet ones are always the most dangerous because it is not about show, but it's about principle, respect and integrity. Those same principles also apply to competitors in your marketplace. While your focus should always remain on your customer and not your competition, it doesn't mean you should take them for granted.

From experiences with Nike, I remember watching the launch of Under Armour as a sports brand. While most of us recognized their existence in the marketplace, it did not preoccupy our time, as our strategies were focused on our points of differentiation as the market leader. However through the years they have continued their on-field pursuits and are now a global brand with revenues in excess of $2.3 billion.

"I never underestimate my opponent, but I never underestimate my talents."

- Hale Irwin

Six on Leadership

Remember the Renaissance

Be a Renaissance Man!

Six on Leadership

The Renaissance was the transition between medieval times and modern civilization. You must learn to become the Ying and the Yang (balanced in all aspects of your business and personal life). You have to be as comfortable escorting a client to the corporate boardroom, or down the "Red Carpet," as you are capable of handling your business during an attack on principal. You have to become a modern day Renaissance man.

You must be able to understand and appreciate. In many cases, you must assimilate into multiple cultures and environments. We live in a big diverse, borderless world. Celebrating our diversity doesn't mean we can't debate our differences, it just means a person's ethnicity does not have to be a factor in the discussion.

With the continued growth of social media we are no longer separated by six degrees. We are often separated by only two or three. Sometimes that separation may only be a few key strokes in a search engine. As a leader we must also understand our online persona can not only connect us with the world, it can also limit or restrict the success of our organization if we find our views are not respectful, inclusive or may be alienating.

Chapter 3

Six on Life

"To whom much is given, much is required."
Luke 12:48

Six on Life

I think it is fundamentally and morally impossible for a man or a woman to work hard to build a successful organization or corporation and not make an attempt to help build a better society. As leadership is not a trait we turn on and off, but a mindset and characteristic that permeates our being.

Whether through environmental sustainability, alternative energy/clean tech programs, or various social enrichment initiatives to benefit employees, customers or the community at large. Corporate citizenship is not about reducing liability it's about taking responsibility.

Simplify Your Life

In the early 80's Eddie Murphy and Dan Aykroyd did a comedy entitled "Trading Places" where an upper class commodities broker and a street hustler cross paths and the commodities broker gets a taste of homeless life. And like so many others falls victim to the phrase, *"Desperation is often the source of poor decisions." -- Patique Collins*

Whether as a result of the decline of the housing market, loss of employment, or the result of excessive workloads on our existing jobs, many people are finding themselves overextended either emotionally, financially or physically. Unless we learn to simplify our lives, stop feeling so compelled to live above our means and stop trying to keep up with the Joneses we will continue to be that hamster on the wheel.

We all come from different places and circumstances, but where we start our journey in life is not where we have to end. Rich is as much a state of mind as it is a financial statement. When you learn to

Six on Life

simplify your life, you will find your gifts are in abundance.

Too often in life we spend so much time working that we never stop to enjoy the fruits of our labor. What you do for a living doesn't have to constitute your lifestyle. I now make it a habit when I travel, to get up early in the morning and experience life undisturbed. Whether it is a walk on the beach, a dip in the pool or a lounge chair on the roof enjoying the skyline, there is nothing like the joy of inner peace and personal reflection.

On a recent business trip to the south of France, I stayed at a very luxurious hotel. What I remember most about the trip was getting up early in the morning and walking on the beach before the locals and the tourists started their sunbathing routine. The sky was pastel blue, the water was pantone, the sun was burnt orange and set right on the horizon, the air was salty, the sand was heavy and the mornings were peaceful. I can't remember the color of my room, what floor I was on, or what I had for breakfast, lunch or dinner.

It was a productive trip, my client thanked me for the service and I still remember, the sky was pastel blue, the water was pantone, the sun was burnt orange and set right on the horizon, the air was salty, the sand was heavy and the mornings were peaceful.

Six on Life

Life is pretty simple. Wake up each morning and try to be a better person today than the one you were yesterday.

Six on Life

Don't Run Out of Runway

"Don't Run Out of Runway."
Frank Heath

Six on Life

At some point in all of our lives, we reach a point of stagnation, plateau or comfort. Whether it is the result of signing a large contract, large lump sum payout (severance package, insurance settlement or lottery winning) or other windfall, eventually all good things will come to an end.

Stay busy. Always maintain a sense of urgency and purpose. Focus on developing multiple "what if" scenarios in your go-forward strategy as you prepare for the next juncture in your life. Your plans should always be built on lowest performing Performa. Despite what you think from the point of conception to the actual point of implementation and execution, the timing is always longer than you anticipate.

The best time to start working on that plan is right now. The longer you wait, the longer you risk running out of runway and never allowing your idea or the opportunity to take off.

Just remember, planning is a passive action. Until the plan actually goes into implementation it is just another great idea. In the words of General George Patton, *"A good plan violently executed right now, is better than a perfect plan executed next week."*

Six on Life

Society will continue to remain morally bankrupt as long as good people continue to sit idly by and allow hate mongers to make emotional withdrawals.

We must avoid becoming a culture of intolerance or inaction. Two of the greatest disservices to society are the creation of the garage and the virtual privacy fence. The garage allows us to come home, drive in and ignore that which lives right outside our front door.

The virtual privacy fence is the invisible barrier inside of our head that allows us to tolerate injustice and pretend it does not exist, because it is not happening directly to us. However, we can never have a polite society when another man's family lives in hunger, fear or despair.

Six on Life

We can't create a better society if we are more committed to being a collection of individual family units than a community.

Society will continue to remain morally bankrupt as long as good people continue to sit idly by and allow hate mongers to make emotional withdrawals. If we never make deposits of love and compassion then what will our kids have to draw upon.

Edmund Burke once said, "The only thing necessary for the triumph of evil is that good men do nothing."

Six on Life

Defining Character

Character is our personal dictionary, it defines our life.

The character of a man lies deep inside his soul. It can't be blown away by the wind, washed away by the tide, swayed by group consensus or paid for by the highest bidder.

It resonates from his faith, is forged by his life experiences and polished by the choices he makes. His character manifests itself more by what he won't stand for than what he does. He is a quiet man of honor.

89

Six on Life

There is no such thing as a character building moment, there are only character revealing moments.

"Nearly all men can stand adversity, but if you want to test a man's character, give him power."

- Abraham Lincoln

Six on Life

Understanding Vigilance

Vigilance isn't a discipline, it is a requirement. Around the corner or around the world, it transcends cultures, languages, events or activities.

Every year for high school graduation parents around the world gift their children with overseas graduation trips to celebrate their recent milestone. Despite their best intentions, how prepared are our kids to travel around the world to a new culture, new language and often dramatically different environment?

Six on Life

Most of those kids have had the luxury of their parents providing the guardrails to channel their behavior for the majority of their lives. Many have had mom or dad regularly traveling with them or were just a phone call away, always there to be the first or last line of defense.

Now take that same young man or young woman post-graduation who is now coming into the height of their sexuality and remove all of the guardrails. While most of us have taught our children to be trusting, professional predators often rely on that level of trust and naivety to compromise their targets.

One of the greatest gifts we can give our loved ones is the gift of situational awareness. Teaching them to understand what belongs and what is out of place. Learning to trust their instincts. Situational awareness is more than just staying in tune with your environment it is learning to stay in the moment at all times.

Six on Life

As Robert De Niro said in the movie Ronin, *"If you have any doubt there is no doubt."*

Vigilance is the discipline of situational awareness. Therefore it isn't just a discipline it is a requirement. It is a skill that protection specialists and everyday citizens should use to travel whether around the corner or around the world. It transcends cultures, languages, events or activities.

As a business unit leader or professional business traveler what are you doing to enhance your personal safety or that of your employees when either of you travel locally or abroad?

Six on Life

Walk in My Shoes

If you have never walked in my shoes you can't begin to understand the pain in my feet.

As you continue to grow and succeed in your career you will develop detractors or haters. As George Bernard Shaw reminds us, *"Hatred is the cowards answer to being intimidated."*

They will often question why or how you got there. They will never be aware of all the sacrifices and obstacles you had to overcome in order to get to where you are today. They are the validation you are on the right track.

94

Six on Life

"Never waste your time trying to explain who you are to people who are committed to misunderstanding you."
Unknown

Most of them are not in a position to hire you or positively impact your success. What they are actually reflecting is their own insecurities. Also, avoid wasting time with people who are intellectually lazy. You can't have a logical discussion with people who are devoid of logic and common sense.

The pain from your struggle was God's way of stress testing you, to prepare you for your success. There can never be a testimony without first the test.

Six on Life

Never Pass Judgment

You should never attempt to pass judgment on a man or a woman based on a single interaction. However, the collection of their words and actions will tell you a lot about their character. It is through the understanding of their character that the actual person is revealed.

Six on Life

Don't profile or prejudge. Learn to focus on people's behaviors and determine whether their actions are consistent with their words. Their character will be validated by the collection of their actions. Understanding character is like putting a jigsaw puzzle together. With just a piece or two you can't quite understand the picture, but once you put together several pieces, the picture starts to become pretty clear.

Six on Life

Understanding Change

History has taught us that change is inevitable. The only question is will it come by evolution or revolution? The speed and sense of urgency is historically dictated by a society's pain, emotional capital or moral fiber.

Six on Life

There is often tremendous anxiety for some when they contemplate change. However, change in and of itself is neutral. The anxiety comes from not understanding how that change will impact you, your family or your client. Whether it is a change in employment, change in industry standard or regulation, there are always signs.

Our responsibility is to stay contemporary with the requirements of our job, industry or client expectations. When a client or employer wants to have a change of direction, they won't call you up and ask permission. So your job is to remain relevant, continue to provide value added services and keep your skills contemporary with the needs of the industry, your employer or your client.

As a manager, to avoid the disruptions and natural anxiety often created by change, make sure you provide clear feedback to your employees on how they fit into the new reality as this will avoid losses in productivity and morale.

Chapter 4

Six on the Things That Really Matter

*"Give Me My Flowers,
While I Am Living."*

Six on Things That Really Matter

Your Most Important Client

Your business may take you around the world. However, never spend so much time getting stamps on your passport, you forget to stamp home. Extensive travel can be hell on relationships.

Six on Things That Really Matter

What we do for a living doesn't constitute our lifestyle. Just as we provide comfort and value to our clients, we have to also make sure we are taking care of home. The long hours and ongoing travel can be hell on a relationship and family. Before you consider an opportunity with extensive travel make sure your family has full disclosure of the requirements of the job and the sacrifices you all will collectively have to make.

It has been proven many times over direct deposit and perceived glamour of the job is not enough to hold a family or relationship together. If your spouse or significant other has never been blessed with the perceived benefits of travel whether around the corner or around the world, there is the ability to resent your current employment choice. They don't understand there is no joy in long security lines, delayed flights, bad airplane food and smaller seats. You are up before your clients, and you go to bed after your clients. But remember, your family's perception is their reality. So, that is all that matters.

If your job is not security focused, consider redeeming some of those frequent flyer miles and you and your spouse or significant other fly in a day or two before the business trip so you can spend some quality time together. You have just cut the cost of your vacation by half or more as you only had to pay for logging cost for the incremental days. You probably also have frequent traveler hotel room nights available, so there may not even be a cost for the room for the incremental nights.

If you can't bring your loved one along consider using Skype or FaceTime or other internet video chat services so you can connect face to face. If you can't connect face to face, the good ol' surprise

Six on Things That Really Matter

post card from afar is another way to let them know they are on your mind. When you get back home, don't forget to take some personal time with those you love. Not only do they want to hear about your trip, they genuinely want to see you and tell you what has been happening in their lives. Show the same genuine interest in things going on in their worlds as what is happening in yours.

Your most important clients and your true inner circle are the family you leave behind when you grab your go-bag. If things are out of balance at home, it will filter over into your assignment. It will manifest itself in lack of focus, loss of attention to detail, lack of sleep, service failures with your client and lack of adherence to your normal safety protocols or operation procedures. Never be so focused on getting stamps on your passport that you miss stamping the most critical destination called home.

Six on Things That Really Matter

Parents, when raising our children, we must be careful as to foster expectation versus entitlement. One promotes growth, while the other encourages dependence.

As a parent, it is our moral obligation to provide for our children. It is also only natural that each generation desires to pass on or provide more for their children than they had for themselves.

Education as an expectation was a part of my family dynamics. That reality originated with my grandmother's years of service as an educator. It was probably the greatest family heirloom that could have been passed down. When it came to grades there was an

Six on Things That Really Matter

expectation that we would do well. I remember my dad saying, "Your last name is James; you are not below average in anything." So, it was expected that mindset would translate into academic performance. It did. It wasn't that he expected us to always make straight A's, but he expected us to always apply ourselves fully and to understand that we had the mental capacity for excellence if we incorporated that little thing called work ethic.

I tried to share that same lesson with my own daughter not because I wanted it for me, but I wanted her to understand that a great education would give her more options in life to do whatever she desired. I am pleased to say she was a phenomenal student and she has a great work ethic today.

One of the greatest challenges I see today is many parents have stopped teaching and have defined parenting by their ability to provide material things to their kids as opposed to sharing life lessons that are both timeless and priceless. We are developing an entitlement mentality in our current generation, which does not seem to understand the only place where success comes before work is in the dictionary.

Parents, when raising our children we must be careful as to foster expectation versus entitlement. One promotes growth, while the other encourages dependence.

I remember as my daughter got older, we continued to give her responsibilities as ways to earn her allowance. When she turned 13, her mom and I sat down and looked at her monthly requirements and requests, including clothes, extra circular activities and entertainment. We established a budget for her then we started giving her a monthly

Six on Things That Really Matter

allowance.

The first month she ran out of money at the end of the second week. The second month she made it to week three. By the third month, she had learned to reconcile wants and desires with the money she had earned. You can never teach a child to budget if you never give them a budget.

As she grew older and started working outside the home, she learned that if she wanted things in life, she had to be prepared to work hard to get them. The best way to control your destination is the take initiative and give yourself options. Those are life skills that will serve her forever.

Frederick Douglass once said, *"It is easier to build strong children than to repair broken men."*

Six on Things That Really Matter

The Walk

The time will come when you realize your daughter is all grown up, but you can still cherish the fact that she will always be a daddy's girl. There is nothing more precious than the love between a father and his daughter.

Six on Things That Really Matter

A father can never teach his daughter how to be a woman, but he can teach her what she should look for in a man. As a father you are the first man she will ever love. You provide her comfort and security that things will always be okay no matter what goes on in her life. You are her alpha and her omega. You are her first and last line of defense. You are the key to unlocking her beauty inside and out. You are the primary stimulus in the growth and development of her self-esteem. You can never tell her she is the most beautiful and cherished young lady enough. Cherish the moments. Celebrate every special day:

- Birthdays
- Baptisms
- Competitions
- Recitals
- Engagements
- Graduations
- Valentine's Day

As a business leader, your business should be able to sustain itself in your absence. If you cannot afford to leave the office early or preschedule a day off months in advance to celebrate a special day, then you are missing one of the critical core competencies as a leader, the development of your team and making your actions scale.

While I only have one child, a daughter, I was very instrumental in the raising of my nephew. So I share the same passion for the impact of a father or uncle on the development of their son, grandson or nephew.

As a man, your job is to impart the life lessons on how to be a man.

Six on Things That Really Matter

A prince can only learn how to be a king from watching a king. The young man you are influencing needs to experience both love and discipline. You can never *tell* him how to be a man, you can only *show* him how to be a man. You don't tell him to respect women, you let him watch you open doors for ladies.

It is not to say that you and the significant woman in your life won't have challenges from time to time, you just show him that the two of you can find more harmonious ways to discuss your differences. You teach him, how to be a good provider by first showing him what a good work ethic looks like, and what it means to be the head of the household. I remember as a young man, whenever I wanted a major item in my life, whether it was a new bike, motorcycle or car, my dad was always supportive. He still made me work to save my money and said when I could pay half, he would have the other half. That taught me about working, budgeting and saving money. Also when you work hard to earn something, you are much more inclined to take care of it.

Clients will come and go but we only have one family and we will never have another opportunity to capture those important moments in our children's lives. While they may always smile and say mom or dad it's okay, deep down when the other kids had their parents around, they missed you. If you miss the significant moments in their lives, when a crisis or emergency arises you have taught them to seek shelter elsewhere as you have not been there for them. The most important job we will ever have in our lives is the development and support of our children. Never let your job, make you lose focus on the things that really matter.

Six on Things That Really Matter

Health and Wellness

Health and wellness is a lifestyle. It is not a diet or an exercise program.

The only thing consistent about extensive travel is that it is consistently inconsistent. The hours are often long. We are up before everyone else and go to bed after everyone else. If you have global responsibility it is always 9:00am – 5:00pm somewhere in the world. So, often your sleeping patterns can become altered. By the time we start or end our day, many times the quality eating establishments may be closed.

Six on Things That Really Matter

We often allow our jobs to become a convenient reason to not take care of ourselves. Growing up, I played football, baseball, basketball and I wrestled and had always lived an active lifestyle. Then as my career began to advance, my lifestyle unfortunately became more sedentary. One day I was sitting down with a good friend and we were discussing how his father-in-law had recently moved in with him and his wife and that his father-in-law's health was starting to deteriorate.

When he and his wife first met, his father-in-law was our age. Unfortunately, through the years he had not taken the best care of himself and it was catching up with him. Since I knew high blood pressure ran in my family, I then made a decision that was a family legacy I was going to change.

Through one of my clients, I met a phenomenal trainer Jason Van Heulen who encouraged me to think lifestyle not quick fix. From observing my work ethic, he knew all he had to do was get me started and the rest would take care of itself.

We focused on changing my eating habits and letting the exercise come on its own. Needless to say it worked and success is its own motivator. I am in as good of shape as when I was 20 years younger. My vitals are in great shape and my blood pressure and resting pulse are in the same zone as high performing athlete.

I now encourage everyone to make health and wellness their goal by learning to maintain a healthy and balanced diet, get plenty of rest and exercise regularly. While everyone has different nutrition needs, I like to focus on a diet that consists of 50% protein, 30% carbohydrates and 20% good fats from foods like olive oil, coconut oil or nuts.

Six on Things That Really Matter

Avoid foods and snacks that artificially spike the blood sugar. While they may provide you temporary energy, the after crash can be brutal.

When quality food is at a premium or you are time challenged consider protein shakes, power bars, fruits and nuts to help supplement your nutrition plans. Try to avoid protein bars with sugar and stay away from the energy drinks whenever possible as most are high in sugar. When traveling, I prefer individual protein mix packets as opposed to large containers and multi serving packs. Most trips are not long enough for you to use the entire container or package and I would hate for a TSA to make you throw away a $35 - $50 container of opened protein mix. Also, when I travel abroad, if I am not a fan of the local cuisine the protein shakes provide a great meal replacement option.

You don't have to join an expense fitness center to stay in shape. Buy a resistance band and jump rope and leave them in your travel bags. They will provide you a 24-hour gym on the go. Between body weight exercises, like push-ups, sit ups, planks, squats will provide you a great workout until you get back home. A regular exercise routine has proven to lower blood pressure, reduce stress and aid in helping enhance sleep without the side effects of medication.

Why do I try to maintain a healthy lifestyle? Because I want to be around for my family for a long time. For the more vain, Jayne Cox said it best, "It is easier to wake up early and work out than it is to look in the mirror each day and not like what you see."

Six on Things That Really Matter

Get a Dog

"Get a dog. It will make you a better person."

- The Bond

You have always been there for him. You raised him from a puppy. You fed him, played with him, cleaned up after him, and trained him. You gave him love and discipline. You took it slow and inspired confidence in him as you built the bond. You let him know you would not allow any harm to come to him. He now lets you know, he will not allow any harm to come to you either!

Learn to be the good person your dog thinks you are. One of the best things about owning a dog, is no matter your age, religion, economic status, maturity or sexual orientation, your dog could care less, they

Six on Things That Really Matter

will accept you just the way you are. Get a dog. It will make you a better person. Their positive attributes are addicting and most definitely contagious. No matter how smart or intellectually lazy you may be, they will teach you love, patience, compassion, discipline, responsibility and how to have balance in your life. They give you purpose. To quote Will Smith, "When you wake up in the morning and your life means something to somebody (or something – your dog) other than you, that if you don't go do the things you are going to do, people's (or your dogs) lives suffer. Your sense of compassion and responsibility will never want to let them down.

I remember a time early one morning while I was out walking my dog Maximus, I saw this little child (approximately 2 years old) pushing his wagon in our direction. The child dropped the handle of his wagon and proceeded straight toward Maximus. I put Maximus in the down position and commanded him stay. The little kid extended his hand with his index finger leading toward Maximus (scene from the ET movie). This was one of the most compassionate moments I have ever witnessed in my life.

Maximus licked his finger, the child then proceeded to rub Maximus' head then back. Maximus never moved or flinched he just let the child do what he wanted to. The child got on his back. Maximus then rubbed him with his muzzle. After a few moments of play time the little boy's mom said it was time to go. The little boy rubbed Maximus' head again, Maximus again licked his hand. The little boy's mom, almost with tears in her eyes, said thank you.

It was a "We Are the World" moment. Big dog, small child, Asian lady, Black man. Humanity and compassion don't know religion, age,

Six on Things That Really Matter

ethnicity or species. We should all strive to be like our kids and our dogs – accepting and non-judgmental.

One of the great things about owning a dog, is the ability to experience that unconditional love every day. They never have a bad day, they are always happy to see you and you know they always have your back. If you ever have a two legged friend that is as loyal as your four legged friend, you have someone special. So when you hear someone refer to their two legged friend as "that's my dog," understand it truly is a term of endearment.

In business, protective services or life in general, I encourage you to find someone who truly has your six (back) where you can develop that operational chemistry and bond you often see with handlers and their K-9 partners. Having that operational chemistry and comfort level allows you to increase your protective capabilities and sharpen your focus, as you are 100% confident that your partner has the competencies and loyalty to handle their arch of responsibility or sector of fire and leaves you the ability to focus 100% on your own responsibilities.

In the civilian world it gives you the ability to let your hair down and know no one is watching, evaluating or critiquing. They are just busy loving. Whether they are a friend, spouse or significant other you know they will be with you through thick or thin and truly for better or worse.

Six on Things That Really Matter

You Are Late

You're late for your tee time.

Often in our dedication to our family, career or sense of personal responsibility we find ourselves totally engrossed in our job. Yes you become a workaholic. While the company may appreciate your loyalty and dedication, don't fall for the fallacy the business cannot function in your absence. Have your first work related stroke, heart attack or fall asleep at the wheel late night and have an accident based on your exhaustion. See if the company opens up the next day. The answer, unless you are a solo operator the answer is an astounding,

Six on Things That Really Matter

yes.

When you burn the candle on both ends, it burns twice as bright but half as long. Learn to allow yourself time to recharge the engine. Use your vacation time, you have earned it. Studies have shown unless you allow yourself time to recharge the batteries, you are actually limiting your ability to maximize your performance. As we grow in our careers we stop getting paid by the hour and start getting paid by the output. So complete the project and take some time to clear your head, rest the body and come back fresher than ever. This will increase your capacity and better prepare you for the next big project or task.

You don't have to play golf, but find a hobby you can do on your own. Taking personal time out for yourself, doesn't make you less of a family man or selfish, it just makes you human. We all need a little quality time alone. Find your own personal safe haven that takes your mind totally off your business and get you away from the masses to include the family, even if only for an hour. So take a yoga class, go skiing, go to the woods or go ride that Harley, you will be better for it.

Six on Things That Really Matter

Believe In Something Bigger Than Yourself

Believe in something bigger than yourself.

Six on Things That Really Matter

It has been often said that heroes aren't larger than life, they are just larger than their own lives. If you are reading this book you have already been blessed abundantly by managing your ongoing personal development. This has allowed you to accomplish your goals in life up to this point.

Consider paying it forward. Volunteer at your local food bank. Coach a little league team. Support a local victim's assistance shelter. Make a contribution to your local humane society. Donate those old clothes in your closet to the Red Cross. Stop by your local VA hospital and take a moment to thank a veteran. Be a Big Brother or Big Sister. Volunteer for the Scouts. Set up an internship program at your office. You get where I'm going with this?

It doesn't make any difference how you chose to give back, just be the blessing.

The picture on the prior page is our TM logo for our community service program Angel by Panther Protection Services. We gift situational awareness and self-defense training to victims of domestic violence and residents of victim assistance shelters. Contact Panther Protection Services at info@pantherprotectionservices.com about sponsoring training for a shelter in your area.

Index

Index

About the Author   VIII
Adversity   24
Angel By Panther Protection Services   118
Articulating Your Value   50
Avoid Always Being The Last Line of Defense   48,49
Avoid Passing Judgment   96
Be a Spartan   55
Believe In Something Bigger Than Yourself   118
Brand Positioning   9,10
Brand Synergy   13
Building a Team   23
Building Strong Children   106
Change   98,99
Character   89,90
Characteristics of High Performing Teams   11
Chess Not Checkers   1
Civility   66
Client Centric Culture   16
Complacency   85
Core User   10
Courtesy & Diplomacy   71
Cutting Through the Clutter   31
Dedication   VII
Defining Character   89
Delegation   69,70
Desperation   82
Discounting   35,36
Don't be Afraid to Manage with Courage   59,60,61
Don't Front Money for Millionaires   51
Don't Run Out of Runway   85
Don't Tolerate Insubordination   62,63

Index

Driven to Please	16
Empowerment	49
Enhancing Communication	37
Entrepreneurial Success	17
Exchange Rate	50
Expectation vs. Entitlement	104,105,106
Experience	57
Extended Terms	52
Frame of Reference	10
Get a Dog	113
Give Me My Flowers While I Am Living	100
Haters	94
Health & Wellness	110,111,112
Herding Cats	39
High Performing Organizations	46
Importance of Brand Positioning	12
Intolerance	87
Keep Your Training Business Demand Driven	27,28
Leading from the Front	58
Leveraging Success	22
Long Term Sustainable Results	45
Louis Vitton	11
Managing Group Meetings	39,40
Marketing	31
Marketing Elevates Your Voice	32
Morally Bankrupt	87
Most Important Client	101,102,103
My Personal Action Plan	125
Negativity	62
Never Attempt to Pass Judgment	96
Never Confuse Enthusiasm with Competency	25

Index

Never Miss A Moment   108
Never Underestimate   78
Not My Place   64
Oakley   14,15
OPE   52
OPM   52
Opportunities   4
Pick Up That Piece of Paper   58
Positioning Elements   13
Positioning Statement   10
Professionalism   73
Relationship Chemistry   72,73
Remember the Renaissance   79
Renaissance Man   79,80
Respect   72
Sales   32
Self-Esteem   67
Self Starter   24
Simplify Your Life   82
Situational Awareness   92
Speak Less, Listen More   35
Standards   7,8
Standing Alone   67
Strategic Partnerships   75,76
Strengths   3
SWOT Analysis   3
Team Player   24
The Bond   113
The Uh Huh Moment   20
The Walk   107
Things That Really Matter   100

Index

Threats   4
Understanding Sales vs Marketing   30
Understanding the Positioning Elements   13
Vigilance   91
Walked in My Shoes   94
Weaknesses   4
Why Small Businesses Fail   54
Wisdom   57
Won't Work Out Like You Think   77
You Are Late for That Tee Time   116

Appendix

Appendix

My Personal Action Plan

What are the top 3 takeaways from Six on Business can you apply to your personal business situation?

1.

2.

3.

What are the top 3 takeaways from Six on Leadership can you apply to your personal Leadership style?

1.

2.

3.

Appendix

My Personal Action Plan Continued

What are the top 3 takeaways from Six on Life can you apply to your personal Life style?

1.

2.

3.

What are the top 3 takeaways from Six on Things That Really Matter can you apply to your personal business situation?

1.

2.

3.

Made in United States
Orlando, FL
14 June 2022

18794193R00085